Facts About the Hyrax

By Lisa Strattin

© 2016 Lisa Strattin

Facts for Kids Picture Books by Lisa Strattin

Scissortail Flycatcher, Vol 54

Puff Adder, Vol 55

Giant Anteater, Vol 56

Giant Otter, Vol 57

Western Lowland Gorilla, Vol 58

Great Horned Owl, Vol 59

Greater Sage Grouse, Vol 60

Green Heron, Vol 61

Grey Squirrel, Vol 62

Griffon Vulture, Vol 63

Sign Up for New Release Emails Here

http://lisastrattin.com/subscribe-here

Join the KidCrafts Monthly Program Here

http://KidCraftsByLisa.com

All rights reserved. No part of this book may be reproduced by any means whatsoever without the written permission from the author, except brief portions quoted for purpose of review.

All information in this book has been carefully researched and checked for factual accuracy. However, the author and publisher makes no warranty, express or implied, that the information contained herein is appropriate for every individual, situation or purpose and assume no responsibility for errors or omissions. The reader assumes the risk and full responsibility for all actions, and the author will not be held responsible for any loss or damage, whether consequential, incidental, special or otherwise, that may result from the information presented in this book.

I have relied on my own observations as well as many different sources for this book and I have done my best to check facts and give credit where it is due. In the event that any material is used without proper permission, please contact me so that the oversight can be corrected.

Table of Contents

INTRODUCTION 7

CHARACTERISTICS 9

APPEARANCE 13

LIFE STAGES 15

LIFE SPAN 17

SIZE 19

HABITAT 21

DIET 23

FRIENDS / ENEMIES 25

SUITABILITY AS PETS 27

HYRAX PUZZLE 29

KIDCRAFTS MONTHLY SUBSCRIPTION PROGRAM 30

COLOR ME

INTRODUCTION

The name of the Hyrax has been derived from its *'coney'* appearance. They are also known as dassies. It is tough to tell a Hyrax from another rodent. They look similar to them but seem to be related to elephants and manatees. There are four species of Hyraxes, Rock Hyrax, Yellow- Spotted Rock Hyrax, Western Tree Hyrax and Southern Tree Hyrax. These are all along whole of Africa and Middle East.

COLOR ME

CHARACTERISTICS

The Hyrax cannot tolerate very low temperatures which is why they thrive in Africa and the Middle East. They tend to stick together to keep warm and love to bask in the bright sunlight. Their stomachs have several chambers, very much like cows. They prefer to live together in small groups.

COLOR ME

There is one head of the family, a male, which has the job of defending their whole group. They have toes which feel like padded rubber that help them to climb steep rocks.

COLOR ME

APPEARANCE

They are usually between 11 and 20 inches long, the hind feet of a hyrax have 3 toes each, but the front feet have the rubbery pads on 4 toes that we mentioned already They are very agile. They typically have one long nail that is used as a grooming claw, mostly for scratching themselves. The fur of the Hyrax is light brown to gray in color. Their incisor teeth grow into tusks like elephants, with males generally having longer tusks than the females.

COLOR ME

LIFE STAGES

A female usually has one to three young ones in a litter after carrying them in her womb for seven to eight months. The young ones are born with well-groomed body fur and open eyes. They suckle from their mothers for the first few months. A male breeder becomes very aggressive when looking for a mate. They look for a mate to have a family when they are around 18 months old.

COLOR ME

LIFE SPAN

The average life span of Hyraxes ranges from seven to eight years in wild, but that they can live for ten to twelve years in captivity.

COLOR ME

SIZE

The adults weigh between 8 and 11 pounds on average.

COLOR ME

HABITAT

They live in the Sub-Saharan Africa and Middle East. They survive well in dry, arid regions. They growl, squeal and snort to communicate in the group. A sharp bark indicates apparent danger to warn all of the members of the group. They produce an odor which is used by the males of the group to define their territory.

COLOR ME

DIET

They mostly eat herbs but can also feed on small eggs and some insects. A dominant male who heads a group usually stands guard while the group eating. They also eat fruits roots as well as aromatic leaves.

COLOR ME

FRIENDS / ENEMIES

Humans normally do not hurt Hyraxes, although some people in Africa hunt them for food. Their main enemies are Hyenas, Foxes, Jackals, Eagles and big cats.

COLOR ME

SUITABILITY AS PETS

They are not very suitable to be kept as pet because they thrive best while in a group in the wild.

Please leave me a review here:

http://lisastrattin.com/Review-Vol-69

For more Kindle Downloads Visit Lisa Strattin Author Page on Amazon Author Central

http://amazon.com/author/lisastrattin

To see upcoming titles, visit my website at LisaStrattin.com – all books available on kindle!

http://lisastrattin.com

HYRAX PUZZLE

You can get one by copying and pasting this link into your browser: http://lisastrattin.com/HyraxPuzzle

KIDCRAFTS MONTHLY SUBSCRIPTION PROGRAM

Receive a Kids Craft and a Lisa Strattin Full Color Paperback Book Each Month in Your Mailbox!

Get yours by copying and pasting this link into your browser

http://KidCraftsByLisa.com

Made in the USA
Middletown, DE
05 December 2016